The Hour of Departure

poems by

Sonja de Vries

Finishing Line Press
Georgetown, Kentucky

The Hour of Departure

Copyright © 2019 by Sonja de Vries
ISBN 978-1-63534-820-0 First Edition
All rights reserved under International and Pan-American Copyright Conventions. No part of this book may be reproduced in any manner whatsoever without written permission from the publisher, except in the case of brief quotations embodied in critical articles and reviews.

ACKNOWLEDGMENTS

"Better Late (sex after forty)," "In Time," and "When The Two Men Came" were published in *A Narrow Fellow*

Thank you to Editors Sheri Wright, Naomi Wallace and Carla Wallace.

Publisher: Leah Maines
Editor: Christen Kincaid
Cover Art: Nadira Wallace
Author Photo: Josie Sinnott
Cover Design: Shadwick Wilde

Printed in the USA on acid-free paper.
Order online: www.finishinglinepress.com
　　　　　also available on amazon.com

Author inquiries and mail orders:
Finishing Line Press
P. O. Box 1626
Georgetown, Kentucky 40324
U. S. A.

Table of Contents

When The Two Men Came 1

Better Late (Sex after Forty) 2

A Cigar In Amsterdam 3

Sitting By The Ohio With A Felon Who Likes Mark Twain 4

The Waking Echo 5

In Time 6

First Casualty 7

A Still Breath 8

While Picking Blueberries at Bryant Farm 9

Grab My Hips 11

Kneeling On The Earth 12

My Particular 13

The Prince 14

The Runner 16

The Hour Of Departure 17

At The End Of You 18

Departure Haiku 19

Absence 20

To The Other Woman 21

The Promise 22

The Year Of Departure 23

"Love is brief: forgetting lasts so long"

Pablo Neruda

When the two men came

to take my father's body away
they were dressed as though ready

for a photo shoot at a men's magazine.
One of them wore a red silk shirt.

They touched my father as if comforting
a sick child and did not speak to each other.

They tucked in the corners of the limp sheets
lifted his bed up, across the threshold, out the door.

Their muscles strained and I could see one of the men
had a tattoo, a bird underneath the red silk

and as I watched them, I felt the sharp curve of desire
rise up and take its' place, next to the dull weight of grief.

Better Late (sex after forty)

I came to it after years of clearing away the debris.
I came to it from the boys who plunged
into the water of my alcoholic blackouts.
After dancing for strangers in fishnets and leather
and years of floating just outside my body.
I came to it with the women who wore their father's ties
like gangsters from the 30's.
I came to it with men who taught me the risk
of skin on skin—a baptism of sweat and semen, the purity of presence.
Sudden and violent like someone who has not had
water for days, I came to it and I drank, I drank.

A Cigar in Amsterdam

As always you leave behind
a t-shirt, grey, soft, something
a baby would pull to it's mouth.

In the dirt of the garden,
the stub of your cigar.
For a moment as coffee

burns through my brain
I think of my grandmother,
who lived here through nazi occupation.

Dividing rations
between her four children
and the people she hid

who disappeared under the floor
at the sound of boots or a knock on the door.

And as the sun hits my hands
I pick up the stub of your cigar

and without lighting it, put it to my lips.

Sitting by the Ohio with a Felon who likes Mark Twain

A fallen cottonwood limb barely holds us.
I straddle your lap, press my fingernails into your arms
While you hold me as though if we fall in we might drown.
Your mouth tastes of coffee and tobacco.
Your hand restless on my thigh, you say the scene reminds you of
Huck Finn and Jim escaping down river.
Driftwood knocks the shore, beer bottles bob in the river like plastic ducks
at a county fair. In the distance, we hear the sound of rifle shot.
You touch my face without talking ,
and for one breath, the bars dissolve from your eyes.

The Waking Echo

Handcuffs that are not part of a game.
Guards have come to take you back, away from your daughters
who open their smiles to you again, like wounds.
Away from the men in the half-way house
who have become your brothers. Their hands are still shaking
from withdrawal, late night confessions
and the tawdry tales that stand in for the whiskey.

Shaved head, six foot two and tattooed, you look the part in sleep.
In prison, tenderness can get you killed or worse.
And I am thinking of your voice before we slept,
when you sang to me because you
you had hurt me in the dark. It had been an accident.
But it was the moment I understood,
we had gone beyond skin and into blood.

In Time

Hawks circle overhead.
My winter white body
Imprints on a blanket wet
With leaves and rain.
Your hand almost conceals
My hip bone.
My mouth opens.

The hawks cry out.
A whiff of coyote piss
Is released by the heat of the sun.
A lady slipper emerges
Through dead leaves.

Your breath sharp and even
You move like an athlete
A light sheen across your brown chest
As you yell "god damn"
And the woods go silent.

Sparrows chase the hawks into the field.

First casualty

First flight awkward and unbalanced,
She stayed low to the ground.

Beak open wide enough to see the inside
Of her throat, empty and loud.

My son fed her worms he found
Under rocks and in the compost.

Later, shirt off, sculpted muscles
Gleaming like some demi- god

I watched you mow, cut grass like confetti,
A celebration of our short time together.

Later we would find the baby Robin,
Beak cut clean in half, but still open.

And we would pretend it was a mystery.

A Still breath

Driving to the hospital, you told me
your father hid gems in the creek
so you could find them,
Rushed home from his job as a salesman
to practice catch.

He was older than the others.
He took pictures of hummingbirds,
taught you to love the woods.

Not even prison or meth
kept you from writing him a poem
on father's day
and when you were gone,
he would stop to rest his hand on the words.

In May your father was
struck silent and you kneeled before him.
Your thick arms a circle around his body.

It was when I saw you
kiss the top of his head
I knew
the kind of man
you could be.

While Picking Blueberries at Bryant Farm in New Salisbury, Indiana My Husband Disappears.

It is ten minutes, at most.
I can not find him.
Fingers purpled and sticky,

My mouth full of berries,
Greedy, picking,
I barely look up

And then, when I do,
He is gone.
I scan the rows of bushes.

A man his size is impossible
To lose.

But I cannot see him.
I call out.
Turn slow, in a circle.

By the second turn, I know
His heart has stopped
And I will find him,

Crumpled, breathless,
Between the thickets of berries.
I see the years stretch out before me.

I hear myself assure his three daughters
Of his love for them. I show them
The letters he had written.

His daughters will come to know their father,
Through me.
I see myself

Alone.

Picking up strangers every few months,
Not bothering with names.

And the unbearable moment
That will repeat
Each morning when I wake up,

without him.

And then, he is there, striding toward me,
Out from the shadow where he lay, resting.
Red faced and whole, his bucket heavy with berries.

Grab my hips

like you mean it
like you're holding on
to something
that won't give way-
two solid apostrophe's-
and in the middle
this moment of flesh.

Kneeling on the earth

sun-warmed flesh
cupped in my hand
grazing my lips
I take the skin
in my teeth
tease slippery flesh
until I feel
thick slickness
on my tongue
and I swallow the persimmon
whole.

My Particular

He said he could always
find me in a crowd
He said I had a particular
gait, a lilt. He made me
almost glad for my short leg.
And so I felt kinder towards it at night
when i bathed and when I smoothed
scented lotion into my skin,
I took extra time as he would have,
murmuring sweet words from my thigh
all the way down to my toes.
This leg I used to drag behind me,
covered in long skirts, this leg,
now tingling, now shining.

The Prince

We were twins,
born a year apart,
that's what our mother said.

At night we were feral,
left to fend for ourselves
in a wilderness of unwanted

touch and abasement.
In an old photo we lie,
side by

side in a hammock,
a black rat-snake draped
across our bodies.

As teens we lived alone together,
surviving wrecked cars,
cold rage and whiskey.

My girlfriends thought you were
a prince, as you dashed into the night,
your hair like two wings.

But I left for another city
where I chased women and got sober.
You stayed, raced stock cars, burning

figure eights as the crowds screamed.
When I'd visit, sometimes you wouldn't
open the door. When you did, we'd wade

the shallows of Harrods Creek,
our shadows sliding in unison
across the water.

Then came the years of silence
until your stroke brought me back to you.
Thin and quiet you lay in a blue

hospital gown as your beautiful wife
sat looking out the window.
My brother, in those last weeks,

what I held on to: Once you taught me
where to find morel mushrooms.
Once you let me pick persimmons
at the end of your lane

Once
you found me a snake so small
it fit into the palm of my hand.

The Runner

When we were teenagers
my brother drove a pick up truck
daring the road to buck
like the wild ponies we rode as children.
Later he raced in jacked-up cars
with sweaty faced boys
who drank too much and never
talked about their mothers.

My brother was nascar fast,
breaking his neck
to see what was around
that next corner,
flipping, catching fire,
then deciding to race with only
his body to protect him,
his legs more elegant and beautiful
than any I'd seen on a man before.

These are the things I remember
when they find him two days dead from heroin:

how he always wanted
to keep moving.

The hour of departure

The wind tasted like your eyes.
It was as if the door burst into blue flames.
Your body, ice under my hand, my voice only a whisper.
You took the car and the money, not the dog, not the child.
Tyrone was locked up again in Tennessee, this time for life.
I could sing like Patsy Cline. If I were her.

It was February. No one knows the exact day my brother died.
You waited for his death to pass, so you could go too.
You were older than you'd ever been while fentanyl hid
my desire in a bottle with a screw on cap.
That year I was as happy as a child in a bank.
We fell through the garden holding onto Hibiscus.
You were going to miss
those three words.

You left no footprints.
I will forget that you have gone.
Habibi.
Even as the sky drops into my lap.
Even as the ground opens up.

At the End of You

Wrapped inside the red bed sheet,
I found a sock. One of your hiking socks.
Your feet, the only part of you that was simply human.
The rest of you so magnificent at times you left me speechless.
But your feet—you called them frog feet— were evidence
you were part amphibian. They frightened me—not their strangeness—
but their fragility: white, small for your size,
little monsters over the edge of a prison bed.
So you said.
Now I miss them. I did not know it was possible
for longing to pin me to our bed.

Departure Haiku

The Hibiscus climbs
tall as my husband. Springtime.
What is left, flowers.

Absence

The first night
I kept my clothes on.
I could not stand
To feel my own skin
without him.

To The Other Woman

Before he walks out
leaving your children bereft and confused,
before he empties your joint bank account
and takes the car,
he will tell you
he has never loved anyone
the way he loves you.

And he will mean it.

Before he turns away from you
he will make you laugh until you hurt
he will write you things that take your breath
he will surprise you
He will make you want things
you did not know
you could want.

And if you look at him, and really see him,
he may even sing.

The promise

All night I watch the ocean
receding from shells sea creatures
gasping for a breath of salt water
Jellyfish lost to their elegant dance
stranded and heavy with sand
bits of green and blue glass
shreds of garbage exposed

But morning comes
with it's release of the tides
the water carries sea weed and starfish back to life
the shore disappears
the waves rise to meet me.

The Year of Departure

I have watched the deep yellow lilies
push up against the cold watched
the Hibiscus we planted bloom

for the first time I have watched the Catalpa tree
shed its leaves and I have climbed
the roof to find them I have taken men

into my bed sometimes two at a time
leaving their names on the door step
I have learned to live with less

I have walked next to mothers
who lost children I have traded
my wedding ring at a pawn shop

for cash and a blood red garnet
I have danced until my legs ached
said yes and yes and yes

left NO at home on the floor
I have walked two hundred miles
through mountains and watched

a Timber rattler slide across stones
I have seen bare branches glitter with ice

I have lived past you

Sonja de Vries is a queer poet and social justice activist, living in Louisville, Kentucky. She is also an avid photographer. De Vries works as a freelance facilitator of poetry for empowerment and healing with Veterans, Youth and Others as well as teaching and stocking groceries at her local Kroger. Her previous work includes *Planting A Garden In Baghdad* and *Stealing Lorca's Bones,* published by Finishing Line Press. In addition to her work as a writer, De Vries directed several award winning documentaries which have aired on PBS, including *Gay Cuba* and *Out: The Making of A Revolutionary.*

www.ingramcontent.com/pod-product-compliance
Lightning Source LLC
LaVergne TN
LVHW041520070426
835507LV00012B/1711